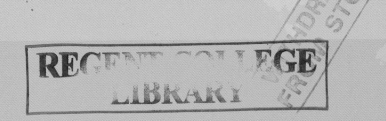

DEVELOPING WORLD

INDIA AND MUMBAI

JENNY VAUGHAN

W

FRANKLIN WATTS
LONDON•SYDNEY

DEVELOPING WORLD

INDIA AND MUMBAI

W

FRANKLIN WATTS

LONDON•SYDNEY

First published in 2013 by
Franklin Watts
338 Euston Road
London
NW1 3BH

Franklin Watts Australia
Level 17/207 Kent Street
Sydney
NSW 2000

HB ISBN 978 1 4451 2360 8
eBook ISBN 978 14451 2366 0
Dewey number: 954.0532

A CIP catalogue record for this book is
available from the British Library.

Series Editor: Julia Bird
Series Advisor: Emma Epsley, geography teacher and consultant
Series Design: sprout.uk.com

Picture credits:

AF Archive/Alamy: 37tl. AJP/Shutterstock: front cover t. Alamy Celebrity/Alamy: 37tr.
arindambanerjee/Shutterstock: 34t.Ajay Bhaskar/Dreamstime 28. Oleg D/Shutterstock: 20.
Dario Diament/Shutterstock: 37b. Excel Media/Rex Features: 13t. Kevin Fletcher/Dreamstime: 38.f9photos/Shutterstock:
43b.Christopher Furlong/Getty Images: 39t. Anna Furman/Shutterstock: 39b. Gauravmasand/Dreamstime: 21b. gopixgo/
Shutterstock: 6. Nick Gray/Wikimedia Commons: 10. Jorg Hackemann/Shutterstock: 26. Nick Hanna/Alamy: 29b. Andrew
Holbrooke/Corbis: 21t.Jaguar PS/Shutterstock: 36. Maurice Joseph/Almay: 27. Lebrecht Music & Arts/Alamy: 35. Lit-
eChoices/Shutterstock: 13b. Kistryn Malgorzata /Shutterstock: 19b. Matt McInnis/Dreamstime: 17t. Vladimir Meinik/Shut-
terstock: 9t. Julia Milberger/istockphoto: 30b. Nice prospects-Prime/Alamy: 29b. OPIS Zagreb/Shutterstock: 30t. Christine
Osborne Pictures/Alamy: 16. Pietrach/Dreamstime: 11t. Plus Lee/Shutterstock: 17b. Paul Prescott/Shutterstock: 22, 31.
Project1photography/Dreamstime: 11c. Jean-Baptiste Rabouan/Alamy: 19t. Daniel Rao/istockphoto: 24. Daniel J. Rao/Shut-
terstock: 25. Fredrik Renander/Alamy: 23. Jeremy Richards/Shutterstock: 33. Samrat35/Dreamstime: 15t, 15b, 40. Sapsiwai/
Shutterstock: 11b. Sipa Press/Rex Features: 12. Nickolay Stanev/Shutterstock: front cover b, 8. Pavel Svobova/Shutterstock:
18. Pal Teravagimov/Shutterstock: 32. Aleksandaar Todorovic/Shutterstock: 21c. View Pictures/UIG/Getty Images: 34b. Ian
Walker/Dreamstime: 7b. World History Archive/Alamy: 9b. Zeber/Shutterstock: 14, 42. Artur Zebrowski/Dreamstime: 41t.

Every effort has been made by the Publishers to ensure that the websites on page 45 of this book are
suitable for children, and that they contain no inappropriate or offensive material. However,
because of the nature of the Internet, it is impossible to guarantee that the contents of these sites
will not be altered. We strongly advise that Internet access is supervised by a responsible adult.

Printed in Malaysia

Franklin Watts is a division of
Hachette Children's Books,
an Hachette UK company.
www.hachette.co.uk

INDIA AND MUMBAI

CONTENTS

LAND OF CONTRASTS

India is the seventh largest country in the world, and covers over three million square kilometres of south Asia. It is a land of huge contrasts. In the far north lies the world's highest mountain range, the Himalayas. Further south, the flat, fertile Indo-Gangetic Plain stretches from Pakistan in the west to Bangladesh in the east, and is made up largely of the Ganga (or Ganges) river basin. The Great Indian (or Thar) Desert forms a southern extension of the plain, stretching into Pakistan. Peninsular India juts out into the Indian Ocean, and has a varied, dramatic landscape with mountain ranges and hills.

The town of Darjiling (formerly Darjeeling) is in the Himalayas. The highest mountain in India, Kanchenjunga, can be seen in the background.

CLIMATE

Climate in India varies from region to region – the mountainous north, for example, has freezing winters, the Thar desert is very dry and the tropical south is lush and wet. India is described as having a 'monsoon climate', which means the seasons depend which way the wind is blowing. From mid-June to early October, winds from the Indian Ocean carry moisture across India, bringing rain. Between November and February, dry winds blow in from the interior of Asia. From March to June, and in October, there is little wind.

A CHANGING COUNTRY

The population of India is growing rapidly. It reached 1.22 billion in 2012. By contrast, when India achieved independence from colonial rule in 1947, the population was just 350 million. Once poor and undeveloped, since the 1990s India has been one of the fastest-growing economies in the world, meaning it produces more goods and services every year. However, while some people have become very wealthy, poverty remains a great problem and an estimated quarter of the population live on less than 40p a day.

TAJIKISTAN
AFGHANISTAN
CHINA
JAMMU & KASHMIR
PAKISTAN
INDO-GANGETIC PLAIN
River Indus
HIMALAYA MOUNTAINS
New Delhi
GREAT INDIAN (THAR) DESERT
River Ganges
NEPAL
EVEREST
Kanchenjunga
Darjiling
BHUTAN
Varanasi
BANGLADESH
I N D I A
Kolkata
BURMA (MYANMAR)
Mumbai
DECCAN PLATEAU
Hyderabad
EASTERN GHATS
Arabian Sea
Goa
WESTERN GHATS
Bay of Bengal
Bangalore
Chennai
INDIAN OCEAN
SRI LANKA

POPULATION GROWTH (2000–2012)

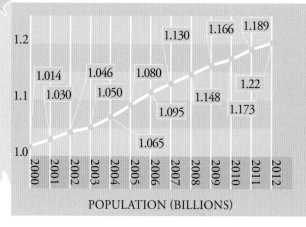

Year	Population (billions)
2000	1.014
2001	1.030
2002	1.046
2003	1.050
2004	1.065
2005	1.080
2006	1.095
2007	1.130
2008	1.148
2009	1.166
2010	1.173
2011	1.22
2012	1.189

POPULATION (BILLIONS)

NEW AND OLD

Rapid development has brought better schools and medical care for many, but has also resulted in pollution, overcrowding and great inequalities between people. However, the traditional values of Indian family life and religion remain important.

India's population growth is largely taking place in its cities, which are growing by around 1.1 per cent each year.

SPOTLIGHT ON INDIA

AREA: 3,287,263 sq km • POPULATION: approx 1.22 billion (2012) • CAPITAL: New Delhi • LARGEST CITIES: Mumbai: 20,500,000; New Delhi: 20,438,946 • LONGEST RIVER: The Ganga (2,510 km) • HIGHEST MOUNTAIN: Kanchenjunga (8,586 metres) • MAIN LANGUAGES: Hindi 41%, Bengali 8.1%, Telugu 7.2%, Marathi 7%, Tamil 5.9%, Urdu 5% • MAIN RELIGIONS: Hindu 80.5%, Muslim 13.4%, Christian 2.3%, Sikh 1.8% • NATURAL RESOURCES: petroleum, coal, natural gas, iron ore, copper, bauxite, ceramic clays, diamonds

PAST INTO PRESENT

ANCIENT INDIA

The first cities on the Indian subcontinent grew up over 4,000 years ago, in present-day Pakistan. India's main religion – now called Hinduism – developed around 3,000 years ago, possibly after settlers arrived from Central Asia.

FOREIGN INVADERS

Between around 320 and 1000 CE, after centuries of being small kingdoms, larger Indian empires grew up. In 1526, Muslim invaders set up the Mughal Empire in India. The British traded with the Mughals through the privately-owned East India Company. This eventually became more powerful than the Mughals, and even had its own army. In 1857, Indian soldiers in this army rebelled. Following this, the British government took direct control of India, though Indians continued to campaign for independence. From 1885, this struggle was led by the Indian National Congress, still a major political party today.

INDEPENDENCE AND AFTERWARDS

India won independence in 1947. With this came the 'partition' of the country into predominantly Hindu India and the largely Muslim Pakistan. As people from both communities fled across the new borders, violence left around a million people dead. Until 1972, Pakistan was divided into two parts: West and East Pakistan, with India located between them. In 1972, following a war between India and Pakistan, East Pakistan became independent Bangladesh – with India's support. West Pakistan remained simply Pakistan.

The Presidential House in New Delhi, designed by British architect Edwin Landseer Lutyens, shows the British legacy in India.

An Indian soldier on duty in Kashmir. Tensions between India and Pakistan, which go back to the partition, are especially acute in this region.

TENSIONS

Although they live in one of the world's fastest-growing economies, many Indians remain poor. This wealth gap dates partly from British rule, when development was designed more to make money for the rulers than the mass of the people. Many Indians also blame governments since independence for mismanaging the economy. Poverty, and tensions between Hindus and Muslims, have made Indian politics volatile, with occasional outbreaks of rioting and violence. Relations between India and Pakistan are strained and war has broken out several times – mostly over the region of Kashmir, which is claimed by both countries. This is especially dangerous, as both countries are now nuclear powers.

MAHATMA GANDHI

PEACEFUL PROTESTOR

Mahatma Gandhi is the most famous campaigner for Indian independence. He was born in 1869 in Gujarat and trained as a lawyer in London. As leader of the Indian National Congress, he led the campaign for independence and was imprisoned as a dangerous rebel, although he always rejected violence. Gandhi opposed the partition of India, and was assassinated by a Hindu extremist in 1948. Gandhi's belief in the importance of non-violent protest lives on today, and he is honoured by peace movements all over the world.

FOCUS ON MUMBAI

ISLAND CITY

Mumbai is the capital of the Indian state of Maharashtra. Originally called Bombay, it grew up on an island with that name off India's west coast. In 1995, the Maharashtra state government officially changed Bombay's name to Mumbai (a name some local people had always used), after a Hindu goddess, Mumba, who is especially important to the city. Re-naming was part of a move throughout India to change place names associated with British rule. Today, Mumbai is India's wealthiest and most populous city.

MUMBAI IN HISTORY

The area around Mumbai has been settled for thousands of years and was an important port as long ago as 1000 BCE. After a brief spell under Portuguese rule, the powerful British East India Company established control over the city. In the 1850s, cotton spinning and weaving mills were set up there. Trade flourished, especially during the US Civil War, when no cotton was exported from the USA, and Mumbai became wealthy.

MUMBAI TODAY

Although textiles are still important, Mumbai is now a centre for many other industries, including metals, chemicals, car-making and electronics. It is also the home of 'Bollywood', India's film hub (see page 36) and is India's financial centre.

CROWDED CITY

Being on an island means Mumbai has always been densely populated. By the end of the 19th century, it was already overcrowded. In the 1950s, it spread northwards after a causeway was built to a neighbouring island, Salsette. Today, the Mumbai Metropolitan Region takes in the city of Mumbai and a number of satellite towns. It is one of the world's most heavily populated cities with over 20 million inhabitants – rocketing up from only around 12 million in 1991. Mumbai's population density is around 30,000 people per square kilometre – believed to be the highest in the world.

The Haji Ali Dargah, a tomb and mosque. This famous Mumbai landmark is visited by people of all religions. It is linked to the city by a causeway and can only be reached at low tide.

A Mumbai street fruit and vegetable market. Mumbai has modern shops and supermarkets, but many people prefer to buy food from open-air markets.

Chowpatty Beach, Mumbai. Mumbai has a number of beaches. This is its best known – and often one of the most crowded.

A group of film extras pose on the set of an Indian-made movie. Mumbai is a centre for movie-making – and is often called 'Bollywood' – a mix of 'Bombay' and 'Hollywood'.

A DIVIDED DEMOCRACY

RIGHT TO VOTE

With 1.22 billion inhabitants, India has over 17 per cent of the world's population. Around one out of six people on this planet live in India. Only China has more people. But India, unlike China, is a democracy – the world's largest. Politicians regularly stand for election to run the country and India's 28 states. The oldest political party is the Indian National Congress. Its main rival, the BJP, is linked to the Hindu religion. Around 700 million Indians have the right to vote: that is anyone over the age of 18 who is not 'mentally challenged' or a criminal.

Indian voters queue at a polling station at the 2009 general election. There were 714 million eligible voters, with 828,804 polling stations.

POWER HOUSE

India has an elected president, but the real power lies with the prime minister, who is the leader of whichever party has the most members of parliament in the Lok Sabha (House of the People). This is one of two houses of parliament. The other is the Rajya Sabha (Council of States), whose members are elected by parliaments in each state.

LANGUAGE

Communication is vital to politics and the economy, but this is made difficult by the fact that India has hundreds of tribal and national groups in India, each with their own languages, dialects and cultures. To make communication easier, Hindi has been made a national language. English, a second official language, is widely spoken in business.

UNEQUAL WEALTH

Although India is home to some of the world's richest people, an estimated one in four people in India is hungry. Poverty is unevenly spread. In the northern state of Bihar in 2010, for example, around 53.5 per cent of people lived in poverty, while in the state of Jammu and Kashmir it was just over 9 per cent. This is partly because some areas have better resources than others. It is also because both foreign and domestic investment favours some parts of India more than others. Deep divisions between rich and poor can encourage resentment, crime and violence.

Children often have to contribute to family income. This girl is collecting cotton waste from a factory to sell for a small price.

WHAT COUNTS AS POOR?

The World Bank measures absolute poverty as less than $1.25 (79p) per day per person to live on. Using this, 2010 poverty levels were estimated as:

- Bangladesh: 43.3% • India: 32.7% • Pakistan: 21%
- China: 13.1% • Mexico: 1.2% (2009)
- Romania: 0.4% (2009)

(No countries in North America or Western Europe had such high levels.)

India's official 2012 measure of poverty is 32 rupees (39p) a day in cities and 26 rupees (31p) a day in villages. This puts numbers living in poverty at under 30 per cent. But critics say India's measure is too low, and that by using more widely accepted measures of $1.25 or $2 a day, the figures would be much higher – possibly as high as 50 per cent.

COMMUNICATIONS

Good communications and transport links are vital in a country as large as India and are all the more important as India grows into a world economic power.

ON THE ROAD

Only around half of all roads – around 1,530,000 km – have hard surfaces. The remainder are unpaved, and are easily damaged in poor weather. However, car ownership in India is growing fast. Back in 2000, fewer than 0.5 per cent of Indians owned a car. Some estimates put this at nearly 5 per cent in 2011.

AIR AND RAIL LINKS

For millions, traditional forms of transport, such as hand-drawn rickshaws and bullock carts, are all that is available. Even public transport is a problem in isolated villages, where a bus stop may be several hours' walk away. By contrast, the better-off can use air travel. India's domestic passenger numbers reached around 60.7 million in 2011 – up 74 per cent from 2006 levels. Rail is important to India's economy, with around 65,000 km of railways, carrying around 7,000 million passengers a year, and over a billion tonnes of freight.

Auto-rickshaws or 'tuk-tuks' are a common sight on India's roads. These three-seater vehicles are very economical to run.

A man in a rural area of Madhya Pradesh state, in central India, talks on a mobile phone. Mobiles are very popular in areas where there are not enough landlines.

India's beautiful beaches attract tourists from all over the world.

KEEPING IN TOUCH

India's first telegraph systems were set up in the 1850s. Landline telephones arrived in the 1880s. However, as in many developing countries, mobile telephones are often more practical than landlines, as they do not need expensive wiring. The first mobile phones reached India in the 1990s, and today there are around a billion subscribers. The Internet is used widely in business. Many homes also have access. People who do not have the Internet at home use Internet cafés.

TOURISM

Mumbai is one the most important of India's seaports, where goods are imported and exported. It also handles more than half of India's international flights. Many of these flights bring tourists – around six million each year, mostly from the US and Europe. In 2010, tourism contributed US $14 billion to India's GDP – over 6 per cent of the total. Tourism can help to support heritage sites, such as ancient temples and wildlife parks, which might otherwise be overlooked in a rush for development. But tourism has its downside: it can damage the environment, use up scarce land and water resources, and have a distorting effect on local culture, as people adapt traditional art and crafts to please visitors.

15

LIVING STANDARDS

When it comes to how people live, there are huge differences between the rich and the poor, like everything else in India.

HEALTHCARE

India has some world-class private hospitals – so good that people from richer countries attend them for treatment, which is often cheaper than in the West. For the poor, there are state-run clinics and programmes for vaccinating children against dangerous diseases, and charities run clinics in the slums and rural areas. But these are not sufficient for India's booming population, and paying for private care – which many Indians must do – can push families into poverty.

A rural vaccination clinic in Goa, India. Indian parents are encouraged to have their babies immunised against a range of diseases, including polio, diphtheria and measles.

ELECTRICITY

As far back as 2003, the Indian government set a goal of providing 'power for all' by 2012, but around 70,000 villages still do not have mains electricity. Even in cities, electricity supplies are not reliable. The country's rapid development has put a great strain on its ageing electricity supply network. As a result, there are frequent power cuts. One in July 2012 left half the country without electricity, bringing public transport and factories to a standstill. The system needs modernising and India needs new power stations. But it is not always easy to get people to agree to these being built – especially when this involves damming rivers for hydroelectric power. There is also the problem of paying for it. Despite its growing wealth, the Indian government has little money to spend, as so many people are too poor to pay much – if any – tax.

WATER AND SANITATION

Millions of Indians do not have access to enough clean drinking water. For example, the 100,000 people or so who live in one slum outside Delhi share just one tap, which is turned on three times a day. One of the biggest dangers to health is from water polluted with human or animal waste – made more likely by the fact that only 15 per cent of people in rural areas have access to a toilet. In city slums, many ditches are open sewers running between the houses. There are encouraging signs, however. In 1990 around 33 per cent of Indians had no access to safe drinking water. By 2008, this was down to 17 per cent. Also in 1990, three quarters of people (75 per cent) in India didn't have access to hygienic toilets. That was reduced to 58 per cent by 2008.

An Indian mother and daughter fetch water at the rural community well in Khuri, a village in Rajasthan.

EDUCATION

Children in Darjiling, in northern India, on their way home from school. In rural areas, children may have to walk several kilometres to and from school.

Good education is essential for any country that wants to compete in the modern world. Providing this is one of greatest challenges facing India.

GOING TO SCHOOL

In 2009, India made education free and compulsory for all children from six to 14. However, not every child gets to go to school. Estimates of those not enrolled in school vary widely – between 5 and 20 per cent – and it is accepted that even enrolled pupils are often absent. In some communities, children may be expected to work instead of study or, in the case of girls,

to help at home. In rural areas, schools are simply too far away for children to reach. By secondary level, estimates of children attending school range from 60 per cent down to 40.

AROUND INDIA

Education levels between states vary. As with fighting poverty, Kerala, in the south, does well, achieving around 90 per cent literacy, compared with about 64 per cent in Bihar. Everywhere, girls fare worse than boys in education as, in many more traditional households, they are held back in education, kept at home and encouraged to marry early.

FOREIGN CAMPUSES

Several foreign universities have set up campuses in India as a means of attracting foreign students (and their fees), without asking them to leave their home countries. These include Leeds Metropolitan University in Bhopal, and Lancaster University, which runs management courses in Delhi. US universities include Virginia Tech, which opened a research centre in Tamil Nadu in 2013.

BRAIN DRAIN

One problem India faces is keeping its most highly qualified people. Many graduates leave for the US, Europe and Australia, where there are better career opportunities and higher wages. For example, a senior scientist in an Indian university might earn around £20,000 a year – but can get four or five times that in the US.

UNIVERSITY AND COLLEGE

India has some high quality universities and colleges, such as the University of Mumbai, whose history goes back over 100 years. These have played an important part in educating India's politicians, scientists and business people over the years. Now the Indian government believes that higher education must expand if India's economy is to go on growing. Around 12 per cent of young Indians go to university, and there are plans to increase this to 30 per cent. Hundreds of new universities and colleges are being set up – some by overseas universities building campuses in India (see panel).

A computer class at Mayo College, Ajmer, in Rajasthan. This private school was founded in 1870 by the British Viceroy (ruler) of India, Lord Mayo, for the sons of Indian princes.

The University of Mumbai, founded in 1857, is one of India's oldest and most important universities.

FOCUS ON MUMBAI

LIVING IN MUMBAI

Life in Mumbai presents many of the same advantages and problems as the rest of India. These play out against the backdrop of a busy, heavily populated, developing city.

HIGH RISE VS SLUMS

A 27-storey house, belonging to a wealthy Indian businessman, stands out against Mumbai's skyline. It is not the only extraordinarily luxurious home in Mumbai, as the city is home to many incredibly rich people. Yet, by contrast, more than 60 per cent of Mumbai's inhabitants live on just a few hundred pounds a year, in crowded slums without clean drinking water or proper sanitation.

A MIDDLE CLASS

Like many other Indian cities, Mumbai has a growing middle class that earns less than those in similar jobs in Europe and the US, but still may be able to afford luxury items such as televisions. Some estimate that as many as 50 million Indians are part of this class, which, if the Indian economy continues to expand at its current rate, could grow by as much as ten times within the next ten years.

Living space is at a premium in Mumbai so rents are high. Many middle-class families still live ageing blocks called 'chawls'. These are often overcrowded and in need of repair, but give extended family members a chance to live close to each other at low rents.

MOVING MILLIONS

Like many Indians, few Mumbaikars (Mumbai people) own cars, but this number is increasing fast, with around 450 new vehicles being registered every day. One consequence is polluted air, as traffic fumes swirl up into the sky. But most people (around 90 per cent) rely on public transport. The local railway transports around eight million commuters a day.

Others use buses and these, like the trains and the roads themselves, are incredibly crowded. Richer travellers may be able to travel by auto-rickshaw. Ferries operate between the islands. A metro system is also being built to help relieve the crowds on the roads and trains.

Yet India remains a land where old and new live side by side, and it is no surprise to see that hand-drawn rickshaws and bullock carts are still commonplace on Mumbai's crowded streets.

Tuk tuks in Mumbai. These vehicles add to the pollution in the city's air, but recently, less polluting engines have been developed to help reduce this problem.

Rush hour on Mumbai's busy commuter trains. Mumbai's suburban train network transports over seven million passengers every day.

Dharavi is a huge Mumbai slum, almost in the centre of the city. Over half a million people live there, mostly in illegal settlements with very poor sanitation.

A luxurious apartment building on Mumbai's exclusive Marine Drive, near Chowpatty Beach. Only the very rich can afford to live in buildings like these.

21

ECONOMIC POWERHOUSE

FULL SPEED AHEAD

India's GDP (Gross Domestic Product – the value of everything it produces) has grown at an average of 7 per cent since 1997. By contrast, in the US and Europe, GDP has barely grown at all. Recently, however, India's growth has begun to slow down.

SWEATSHOPS

Some campaigners accuse India of being the world's sweatshop capital, where children as young as five are employed, often in the textile industry. In 2012, the Indian government gave its support to a plan to make employing anyone under 14 a crime punishable by three years in prison.

PAST AND PRESENT

In the past, India's industry was mostly smallscale, such as pot-making for local use. These industries still exist, but others have become far more important. Textiles – cloth and clothing – make up over a quarter of India's income from exports, and it is the second largest textile producer after China. Major retailers, including labels such as Gucci, Gap and Calvin Klein, use Indian factories. Unfortunately, all over the world, this industry has a bad reputation, often relying on sweatshops, where workers put in long hours for low wages, in overcrowded conditions. The best importers inspect the factories regularly to make sure that conditions are acceptable.

Men at work in a textile factory. This industry provides a great boost to India's exports, but people may work long hours for little pay.

TECHNOLOGICAL REVOLUTION

In the 1990s, the Indian government decided to prioritise the growth of its software industry. To make up for India's often unreliable telephone system, the government invested in high-quality satellite communications. Bangalore (also called Bengaluru) in south India became the main centre of the industry, as it was already a base for electronic companies and research institutions for India's military. The industry soon took off. Today, many multinational electronics companies have Indian design and development centres, and successful Indian companies such as Infosys and Wipro Ltd have grown up and developed alongside huge software multinationals such as Microsoft.

OTHER INDUSTRIES

Tata Motors, a world-leading motor manufacturer, has its head office in Mumbai and factories throughout India. It was set up after World War II to make commercial vehicles, and began making passenger cars in the 1990s, including the Tata Nano, an inexpensive car for the home market. Tata has expanded over the years to take in foreign companies, such as Jaguar LandRover in the UK.

CALLING INDIA

Over the past ten years, India has become a successful base for call centres, as international companies such as banks and mobile phone companies looked to cut costs by employing Indian workers to staff their helpdesks. However, there are signs that this once booming industry is now on the wane, with big global businesses such as the huge banking group Santander, relocating their call centres to their countries of origin to improve customer service. Other countries, such as the Philippines are also beginning to emerge as cheaper call centre hubs.

Two young Information Technology workers in Bangalore. Around a third of India's IT professionals work in Bangalore.

AGRICULTURE

Despite its expanding industrial sector, India is still at heart a rural country, and at least half of all workers are involved in farming. Agriculture makes up around a fifth of India's GDP.

SMALL FARMS

Women picking tea on a plantation in Assam, north-west India. India produces around 30 per cent of the world's tea, employing more than two million people.

Indians spend around 25 per cent of their income on food. Most food comes from smallscale, mainly subsistence farms, where farmers grow food for their families, alongside a little extra to sell. Crops include vegetables, such as rice and corn, fruit, such as bananas and mangoes, and staples such as rice and wheat.

CHANGING WAYS

Until recently, only a few crops, such as tea, coffee and cotton, were major exports. Now, other crops are exported. In Punjab, for example, large amounts of wheat are grown to be sold internationally. In 2010, India produced around 80 million tonnes of wheat, making it the world's third largest producer (after China and the EU) and the seventh largest exporter.

LIVESTOCK

Cattle are sacred to Hindus. Many people keep just a few cows, so although there are few large herds, collectively they amount to two million animals – 15 per cent of all the cattle in the world. They are kept for milk, rather than meat. Poultry is also kept on small farms for eggs and meat.

FISHING

Around 3.5 million people in villages along the Indian coastline earn a living from fishing, and millions more depend on the industry. But it is under threat. As larger, powered craft take over from small boats, there is a serious danger of over-fishing, which could lead to the collapse of fish stocks, making it impossible for fishing communities to survive. Campaigners believe it is vital that the Indian government finds a way to prevent this from happening.

Inland, the government is encouraging fish-farming in areas such as West Bengal, where there is plenty of fresh water. Around three and a half million tonnes of fish is produced in inland India – more than half of it now from farms. In the future, India could expand this three times over.

Fishing off the Malabar coast in south-western India. Today, small traditional fishing boats are facing competition from large mechanised ships.

EMPLOYMENT IN INDIA

India's total workforce is around 478 million. Many people (perhaps as many as 90 per cent) work in the 'informal' sector – that is, outside of government control. This makes it hard to know how many people are employed in different ways, but estimates are:

agriculture 52% • services 34% • industry 14%

FARMING CHALLENGES

Subsistence farming is much more challenging than large-scale agriculture. One stroke of bad luck, such as a flood or drought, or an outbreak of illness among the livestock, and a family or whole community can go hungry.

THE 'GREEN REVOLUTION'

Indian farmers tackle the insecurities they face by adopting more modern farming methods. Many now buy and plant high yielding seeds instead of using grain they have saved from previous years. They also apply chemical fertilisers, as well as using animal dung, to enrich soil, and ox-drawn ploughs are giving way to tractors. This change in farming, which began in the 1960s, is called 'the Green Revolution' and has massively increased food production.

THE DOWNSIDE

New technology is not always good news. Older seed varieties and traditional crops are more resistant to drought and do not cost much to grow. The high price of new seeds and artificial fertilisers can lead farmers into debt and many thousands of farmers have been forced to leave the countryside for the cities to make money.

LAND RIGHTS

Many rural people are Adivasi, descendents of the earliest people to live in India. They may always have lived in an area, but it is hard to prove their right to be there. Big projects such as mines and reservoirs may try to throw them off the land. In 2012, protests forced the Indian government to promise more legal rights and better compensation to people displaced by such projects.

Maize (corn) being transported in Rajasthan, north-west India. Getting food from farms to the people who need it is often a problem, and too often, crops go to waste.

Adivasi women at a market in Orissa, eastern India.

OUR LAND!

Chembakolli village is in the Nilgiri Hills in Tamil Nadu. The people there are Adivasi. In 1988, the people of the Nilgiri Hills joined a campaign to get traditionally held land back, and in 1990, they succeeded. Today, many Chembakolli people are still poor, but they live in concrete houses with good roofs, and the children can go to school. They have their own tea plantation, and sell tea all over the world.

FOCUS ON MUMBAI

WORKING CITY

Indians call Mumbai 'the land of opportunities'. Its history as a trading centre goes back as far as the 1600s, when it exported textiles, jewellery, cotton and rice.

MODERN MUMBAI

Mumbai is the commercial capital of India, and its centre of finance and banking. It is one of the world's top ten centres of commerce and contributes around a quarter of India's industrial output. Many large foreign companies have offices in Mumbai, including the communications and technology giant Siemens.

Other industries include software companies, pharmaceutical manufacturers and 'heavy' industry, such as making products of steel and rubber, while the long tradition of textile and garment manufacture still survives. All this offers work to millions – some in factories and offices, but many others work in the informal sector.

INFORMAL WORK

The informal sector is made up of people the government has little contact with. They do not pay tax and are often self-employed. They may work in workshops making clothing or leather goods, drive rickshaws, or get casual work as labourers. Often, they support families who live far away in the villages. Huge amounts of money can be made in these smaller areas of industry. Some estimate that the annual economic output of the sprawling Dharavi slum could be as much as US$1 billion. Yet for many Dharavi residents, there is little to show for it, although things are beginning, slowly, to improve. This is largely thanks to many years of campaigning among the residents of the slum and people working with them.

High-rise buildings are a way to provide homes for the millions who live in Mumbai. These are luxury flats – too expensive for most people.

Every day in Mumbai, about 5,000 deliverymen carry around 175,000 'tiffin tins' (containers of home-cooked lunches) to factories and offices.

The Mumbai head office of the State Bank of India. This is just one of the major banks in Mumbai.

These pots are made in the Dharavi slum and sold for everyday use all over India.

29

ENVIRONMENTAL COSTS

India's development has brought jobs and wealth to many, but it comes at a cost for the environment.

WATER SHORTAGE

Modern farming methods have helped provide food for India's growing population, but this needs huge amounts of water. In the Punjab region so much water is used to grow wheat and rice that the aquifer (underground water) levels are dropping, affecting vital supplies. Mining and quarrying provide important fuel and building materials, but drain water away. Elsewhere, bridges and dams block rivers. The need for water and hydroelectric power stations has led to more and more dams being built. These are controversial, as land where people once lived and farmed is flooded.

SOIL

Deforestation is a major problem. Often, it is the result of logging – trees being chopped down for timber. Land is also cleared for farming. Poor farming methods, which include using too much chemical fertiliser, can damage the soil, leaving it bare. As it washes away, rivers become clogged up and the dangers of flooding increase. Wind can also blow soil away, creating deserts and ruining crops. Around half of India's land surface is affected by soil loss. For India to continue to develop, it is important to educate farmers to look after the soil. There are a number of government initiatives that are trying to help farmers manage the land better, and there are laws against illegal logging.

The Tehri Dam reservoir in northern India. Although it can produce massive amounts of power and water, the dam has resulted in local people losing their land and livelihoods.

When forests are cut down, wildlife and people who depend on forest plants both suffer. The soil may also be washed away, so that it is no longer good for food production.

WATER POLLUTION

India's rivers are often polluted with chemicals from farms and factories, as well as sewage. The River Ganga, which is sacred to the Hindu religion, is particularly badly affected. It flows for over 2,500 km, supplying water to about 400 million people. Two thirds of the untreated sewage from towns and cities along its banks flows into the river, along with industrial waste. The Indian government has had an action plan since the 1980s to clean up the Ganga. In 2010, the plan's second phase was rolled out. Billions of dollars are to be spent tackling pollution and using the sewage to produce biogas to generate electricity.

AIR

India's rapid development has resulted in a big increase in its greenhouse gas emissions, the gases believed to be responsible for climate change. It is estimated that India's greenhouse gas emissions rose by 58 per cent between 1994 and 2007, making India the fourth largest producer of greenhouse gases after China, the US and the EU. In some cities, such as Delhi, 'green taxes' are being considered to discourage drivers, while public transport and cycle lanes are being improved. This should help reduce both greenhouse gases and air pollution.

Smog hangs over the city of Delhi. Scientists warn that the level of pollution in Delhi is dangerous to people's health.

RELIGION
AND CASTE

For most Indians, religion is an important part of their lives, whichever faith they belong to.

THREAT TO TRADITION

Hinduism is the religion of the largest number of Indians. For devout Hindus, who reject material wealth, rapid development can seem alarming. The fact that India is officially a secular (non-religious) state is only partly accepted by traditionalists. Many view the growing modernisation of everyday life – especially among women (see page 41) – as a threat to long-held beliefs and values.

CASTE

The caste system is a social structure linked to Hinduism. People are born into their caste, which affects every part of their lives – where they live, who they marry, what jobs they do, and more.

Hindu pilgrims bathe in the River Ganga in the holy city of Varanasi in northern India. Devout Hindus hope to visit the city at least once in a lifetime.

Discrimination on the grounds of caste is illegal, but it still happens. It is beginning to break down as India develops, but not fast enough for the 'dalits' (once known as 'untouchables') – the 20 per cent of Indians at the very bottom of the caste system. They have few opportunities and get the most lowly-paid jobs. Dalits make up around 90 per cent of India's poor, who see little of the positive side of Indian development.

ISLAM

Even after independence, when millions fled into Pakistan for safety, many Muslims remained in India. They now make up around 13.5 per cent of the population. Muslims often suffer discrimination in today's India. A high proportion (nearly a quarter in cities) are poor and, like the dalits, are often excluded from India's race to development.

Dalit children at work stitching footballs. Dalits traditionally work in 'impure' jobs, such as with leather (considered unclean because of the association with killing cows), butchery and with waste.

Indian Muslims at prayer at the Jama Masjid, the most important mosque in Old Delhi.

RIVALRY

Rivalry between the Muslims and Hindus is centuries old, dating from the earliest Mughal invasions. The bloodshed at partition stemmed from this rivalry, and made it worse. Both religions have fundamentalist wings, which can inflame inter-communal violence (violence between different communities). One of the worst events in memory took place in 1992, when riots all over India left more than 2,000 people dead after militant Hindus destroyed a mosque in Ayodhya, Uttar Pradesh. There have been many other similar events since, all bringing instability to the country and dividing the population.

FAMILY TIES

For Indians of all religions, family is deeply important. It means that people believe family members must care for each other and share their wealth. But it can also lead to nepotism – unfairly favouring family members in employment and other opportunities. This can be a threat to development, as it may exclude talented people from the economy.

THE ARTS

In the past, Indian art was mainly linked to religion. India's beautiful temples, mosques and other religious monuments still attract millions of visitors every year. India's literature, too, was often rooted in religion.

ARCHITECTURE

By contrast, India today has plenty of fine modern architecture. Much reflects India's role as a rapidly developing, modern country. These include public buildings, airport terminals and innovative office buildings – such as the GMS Grande Palladium in Mumbai. However, experts warn against building too much, too fast. India's infrastructure – its roads and power supply – need to be improved if modern construction is to be a success. Some critics say that it is just as important to find ways to build appropriate, affordable housing in India's crowded cities, where around 19 million people still need adequate homes.

GMS Grande Palladium in Mumbai. This new office block was designed by Malik Architecture – one of the country's top firms of architects.

A scene from the Ramayana is acted out at a theatre in Hyderabad.

THE WRITTEN WORD

Ancient Hindu epics, the *Ramayana*, *Mahabharata* and *Bhagavad Gita* were written around 2,500 years ago, and tell the stories of ancient gods and heroes. They are still read, and made into films, plays and poetry. But in India today much new literature is written in English, and available to readers all over the world. This includes the work of writers such as novelists Salman Rushdie, Anita Desai and Arundhati Roy. All these writers have played an important part in introducing modern India to the rest of the world, while Indian drama is gradually finding its way onto the stages of Europe and the US.

Vasu Dixit, of Indian band Swarathma, performing at the Larmer Tree Festival in the UK in 2010. Swarathma is a folk 'fusion' band based in Bangalore that combines folk tunes and Western sounds.

MUSIC

As with most Indian art, music has a long history, and was first played in temples and palaces. Classical Indian music is still played today, as are traditional instruments such as the sitar. But like so much in India, ancient traditions are now often combined with modern influences to create a unique mix that also includes rock and pop, for example, by adding a modern beat to traditional Hindi songs.

AN INDIAN ARTIST

There are many world-class modern artists and sculptors living and working in India today. Atul Dodiya (born 1959), who was born and lives in Mumbai, studied at the city's Sir Jamsetjee Jeejebhoy School of Art (Sir JJ School of Art). His work includes paintings and installations, often inspired by Mumbai's most famous product – Bollywood films (see page 36).

FOCUS ON MUMBAI

MEDIA GIANT

Mumbai's media industry is huge, with many Indian radio and television stations based there, as well as national and local newspapers.

PRINT AND BROADCASTING

Like other cities, Mumbai has its own magazines and newspapers, as well as local editions of national papers, such as the *Times of India*. It has nine local radio stations, including those belonging to India's national public radio company, Akashvani (also called All India Radio) – one of the world's biggest broadcasters. Radio, which reaches nearly everyone, is especially important in a country where many people cannot read.

Around half of households in Mumbai have a television. Most are served by one of the three main cable networks, together bringing over a hundred television channels to the city, in a range of languages. Doordarshan, the national television broadcaster, has two free terrestrial channels on air.

SPORT AND THE MEDIA

Media plays an important part in India's favourite sport – cricket. This is a multi-million dollar business. The television rights are controlled from Mumbai by the Board of Control for Cricket in India (BCCI) – the world's richest cricket governing body.

Mumbai's own team – the Mumbai Indians – has an estimated three million fans worldwide.

BOLLYWOOD

Perhaps the best-known form of Indian media is its massive film industry, which is set to bring in around US $25 billion in 2014. Bollywood produces hundreds of films each year, and India as a whole produces more films than any other country in the world. These are exported all over the globe, to wherever the 25-million-strong worldwide Indian diaspora (see page 38) live. Many of the films involve music and dance.

Hrithik Roshan is one of the biggest Bollywood stars. Here he is pictured at the Cannes Film Festival, with Uruguayan actress Bárbara Mori.

The 2008 hit film Slumdog Millionaire, set and filmed in Mumbai, brought Indian cinema to a worldwide audience.

World-famous cricketer Sachin Tendulkar in action at the IPL final between the Mumbai Indians and Chennai Super Kings.

A roadside fruit-seller in Mumbai reads one of the city's many newspapers.

INDIA IN THE MODERN WORLD

India's role in the world is changing as its economy, people and culture continue to make more and more of an impact.

THE DIASPORA

The Indian diaspora (people of Indian origin living in other countries) is huge – probably around 25 million. Migration began during British rule, when many poor Indians were encouraged (or forced by extreme poverty) to travel to distant parts of the world. Once there, they were often bound by unfair contracts called 'indentures' to remain, more or less as slaves. As a result, there are longstanding communities of people of Indian origin in Africa, the Caribbean and many other places. These grew as their families joined them.

NEW HOMES

In the 20th century, large numbers of Indians migrated to Britain, the US and Australia. With few opportunities at home, many took the opportunity to settle in wealthier parts of the world, where wages were much higher than at home. The first arrivals were mostly men, but later, their families joined them, and new communities of people of Indian origin grew up.

People of Indian origin living in London celebrate Holi, the Hindu festival of colours.

BIG BUSINESS

India's 100 richest people have amassed around US $250 billion between them. Many operate all over the world, such as Lakshmi Mittal, head of the world's largest steelmaking company, with businesses spread around more than 60 countries. Mittal, who is based in London, is the second richest Indian after Mumbai-based Mukesh Ambani, who has made a fortune in oil and gas. These wealthy businesses grew up in an India that is becoming five or six per cent richer every year. Although this rate has been slowing down, this is still a huge contrast with the economies of Europe and the US, where growth has been very limited. As India's economy expands, many European and American businesses are looking to it as a new market for their goods and services.

This sculpture was designed for the London 2012 Olympics by the Indian-born British sculptor, Anish Kapoor. It was mostly funded by ArcelorMittal, whose chairman is the Indian billionaire, Lakshmi Mittal.

TRADITIONAL BELIEFS

Even while Indian business is booming and India's scientists, writers and other skilled people are making an impact in the world, India remains a land of ancient tradition. As India's people have settled in the rest of the world they have brought with them ancient beliefs, such as their traditional Ayurvedic herbal medicine, and stress-reducing techniques such as meditation and yoga, all of which have become popular in the West.

Yoga originated in India. It is now practised throughout the world, as a means of seeking inner peace.

39

WOMEN IN INDIA

A couple celebrate their marriage in Kolkota, West Bengal. Most Indians still support the traditional belief that a marriage should be arranged by the couple's parents.

As India changes, the position of women in society reflects the divide between long-held tradition and modern development.

SUCCESS STORIES

Many Indian women have made remarkable achievements. A woman – Indira Gandhi – became prime minister as long ago as 1966. India has also had a woman president,

Pratibha Devisingh Patil (2007 to 2012). Indian women have been successful in many other areas of work and industry. India has the largest number of professionally qualified women in the world, with more female doctors, scientists and professors than the United States.

DOWRIES

In Indian society, traditionally, sons are valued more highly than daughters. A boy, it is believed, will support his parents one day, but a girl will join another family on marriage and her in-laws may demand money on marriage (a dowry). Dowries were made illegal in the 1960s, but this has never been strictly enforced. The pressure of providing a dowry drives many families into debt – an estimated 80 per cent of bank loans in India are used to finance dowry demands. There are even cases of brides being murdered for their dowries by greedy in-laws.

GENDER IMBALANCE

At worst, families may opt to abort an unborn daughter rather than face poverty. An estimated six million unborn girls were aborted in India in the last ten years. As a result, in 2011, for every 1,000 boys under the age of six, there were just 914 girls. As well as being a humanitarian tragedy, if this gender imbalance continues, India will suffer as a generation of men will be unable to marry and have families. The Indian government is trying to tackle this by banning doctors from revealing a baby's sex and by subsidising girls' higher education.

SCHOOLING

Girls suffer in education, too. They may leave school early, or be kept at home so often that they fall behind. In 2010, the literacy level among girls was just under 75 per cent, compared with nearly 87 per cent of boys. However, attitudes are changing as people realise that educating girls benefits whole families in terms of health, education and earning power. There is an Indian saying that 'when you educate a woman, you educate a family'.

Education for girls still lags behind boys', but there are many pressure groups, as well as government policies, to encourage parents to send their daughters to school.

ROLE OF WOMEN

There are still tensions about the position of women. Modern Indian women who go out to work may be treated with hostility and even violence by traditionally-minded people (both men and women) who cling to the old belief that they should be treated as the property of their father or husbands.

A SHOCKING STORY

In December 2012, a young woman was raped and murdered on a bus in Delhi. Massive street demonstrations followed as Indians found their voice to protest against violence against women. They protested about the urgent need to solve the problem of overcoming traditional attitudes to women that could allow men to think they could behave like this. Unless this happens, campaigners say, India cannot call itself a modern country.

CHANGING TIMES

Children in Agra. Since 2003, infant mortality in India has dropped from 60 per 1,000 births in 2003 to 44 in 2011, thanks to public education programmes.

India certainly has challenges to tackle, but there are many people working to overcome them, and positive signs for the future.

POPULATION

Some estimate that by 2050, India will have a population of around 1.53 billion. This is challenging, but it could be worse. Population growth is slowing. Back in 1950, Indian women had around six children each. Now that average is slightly less than three. This is largely the result of better healthcare and education.

CORRUPTION

Another enduring problem in India is corruption and the culture of giving bribes, such as businesses paying government officials to give them contracts and people paying public officials to do their jobs properly. It is estimated that about $123 billion was taken out of the Indian economy through corruption between 2001–10. Losing sums this size slows India's development. An anti-corruption movement has taken off, with demonstrations and online protests. In 2012, an anti-corruption political party was established.

THE WAY FORWARD

Indian scientists can play a huge part in making development work. This is what Indian Prime Minister Dr Manmohan Singh said to the Indian Science Congress at the beginning of 2013:

'Faster growth …, more sustainable development based on food and energy security, and socio-economic inclusion made possible by rapid growth of basic social services, such as education and health, are all crucial for defining India's future. Science, technology and innovation all have an important role to play ….'

GREEN TECHNOLOGY

India's development is leading to environmental problems, but much is being done to tackle this, from projects to clean up the River Ganga to the government's recent commitment to reduce India's greenhouse gas emissions. In 2012, it dedicated over £6 billion to sourcing 'green' energy that does not add to greenhouse gases – more than any other major world economy. By doing this, it may help not only itself, but the whole world.

A remote road in Himachal Pradesh, in northern India. Preserving India's unique environment is one of its biggest challenges for the future.

43

GLOSSARY

Adivasi tribes of people descended from those whose ancestors lived in India in prehistoric times. They make up around 8 per cent of the Indian population

agriculture farming

aquifer underground rock that contains water

assassinate to kill someone, usually a public or political figure

Ayurvedic the traditional Hindu system of medicine, using diet, herbal treatment and breathing exercises

brain drain when skilled and educated people leave a country to work abroad, usually for better opportunities or more money

caste a traditional Indian system of dividing up society. The four main castes are: Brahmin (priests), warriors, traders and workers. People outside this system are known as dalits. They were once called 'untouchables'

causeway a raised pathway that crosses water

communications getting things or messages from one place to another. Railways and roads are forms of transport communications. Sending messages by telephone, computer or broadcasting are telecommunications

compulsory required by law

corruption being dishonest in business or in government – for example, by taking bribes

deforestation clearing away of trees

democracy a form of government in which citizens have a say in the decisions that affect their lives

development growing or advancing. A country is often described as developing when it is moving from traditional forms of agriculture and small-scale industry to more modern forms of both

dialect a form of a language found in a certain place, or among certain people. For example, English is a single language, but there are many different dialects of it

diaspora the spread of people away from their country of origin

dowry an amount of money and/or property given by a wife to her husband on marriage

export to sell goods or services to another country

extra someone who appears in the background of a film or TV programme

fertiliser a chemical added to soil to make crops grow better

fish farming to breed fish for sale

freight goods carried in bulk

GDP (Gross Domestic Product) the value of goods and services a country produces

greenhouse gases gases such as carbon dioxide which are believed to contribute to climate change

green technology energy produced in ways that do not harm the environment, such as using wind, water or solar (Sun) power to make electricity

heritage sites somewhere – such as a building, or a forest – that has special importance, for example, because of its beauty or history

hygienic clean; promoting health

import to buy goods or services from another country

Indian National Congress the oldest Indian political party, which has formed most Indian governments since independence

inhabitants the people living in a place

invaders armies that enter another country to try to take it over

literacy the ability to read and write

livestock farm animals

middle class people who are not very rich or very poor. People who run small-and medium-sized businesses and professional people such as doctors are often said to be middle class

migration movement from one place to another

monsoon a major wind system that blows in one direction for a season, and then reverses and blows in the opposite direction. The weather varies according to where the wind is coming from – this is called a monsoon system

nepotism when those with power unfairly favour family and friends

peninsula a piece of land that juts out into the sea

population density the number of people per unit of area

sacred holy

sitar a stringed musical instrument with a long neck and rounded body

slum an overcrowded, dirty area in a town, where very poor people live

staple food the most important foods, ones that people use to make up most of their diet, such as rice

subcontinent a part of a continent that is almost separate from the rest of it

subsidise help to pay for

subsistence farming a type of farming where most of the crop is consumed by the farmer and only a little is sold for profit

sustainable capable of being maintained without using up natural resources. For example, wind is a sustainable source of energy as it will not run out

sweatshop a factory or workshop, especially in the clothing industry, where people work for very long hours for low wages and in poor conditions

tax a compulsory payment to the government, deducted from earnings, sales or property

telegraph a way of sending messages along a wire, using electrical signals

textiles (cloth) the textile industry is industry concerned with clothes, such as weaving, or making clothes

tiffin a word used in India for lunch that is brought from people's homes and delivered to their places of work. It can also mean a snack

unpaved a road that has no hard surface – just a dirt road

US Civil War a war that took place between 1861–65 between the northern and southern states of the US, mostly over the issue of slavery

vaccinating giving an injection of a weak form of a germ carrying a disease. This helps the body fight off the stronger forms of the disease

West historically describes the countries of Europe and the US

yoga exercises designed to promore physical and spiritual wellbeing

FURTHER INFORMATION

BOOKS

Countries in our World: India, Darryl Humble (Franklin Watts, 2013)

DK Eyewitness Travel Guide: India, various authors, (Dorling Kindersley, 2011)

India: People, Place, Culture, History, Philip Wilkinson (Dorling Kindersley, 2008)

WEBSITES

https://www.cia.gov/library/publications/the-world-factbook/geos/in.html
Statistics and backround information about India.

http://travel.nationalgeographic.co.uk/travel/countries/india-guide/
Pictures and articles on ancient and modern India, Indian culture and travel.

http://www.actionaid.org.uk/102789/chembakolli.html
A website about life in the Indian village of Chembakolli.

http://www.bbc.co.uk/news/world-asia-india-18391116
A look at green technology in India.

http://www.guardian.co.uk/world/india
The latest news stories from India.

INDEX